THOUGHTS BEYOND WORDS

APHORISM

DAVUT ERSOY

Thoughts Beyond Words
Aphorism

Copyright © 2022 by Davut Ersoy.

Paperback ISBN: 978-1-63812-144-2
Ebook ISBN: 978-1-63812-145-9

All rights reserved. No part in this book may be produced and transmitted in any form or by any means, electronic, or mechanical, including photocopying, recording, or by any information storage and retrieval system, without permission in writing from the copyright owner.

The views expressed in this work are solely those of the author and do not necessarily reflect the views of the publisher hereby disclaims any responsibility for them.

Published by Pen Culture Solutions   01/07/2022

Pen Culture Solutions
1-888-727-7204 (USA)
1-800-950-458 (Australia)
support@penculturesolutions.com

- Life is a journey planned; towards an eternal end.

- One may not remember the surname of his sister, however, if he cannot remember his brother's, this may be a sign of dementia.

- A single ignorant person includes the characteristic of all ignorant people.

- Any of dead face can't be fake.

- You raise your child with your hands, yet he never grows in your eyes.

- Darkness darkens places where light does not illuminate. Nature does not accept emptiness.

- The number one player of each team is the goalkeeper.

- Provided that one's coming isn't known also his departure won't be known.

- Be a person who adds life to life, but don't be a person who stealing your life.

- Life is not an option, however, lifestyle is an option.

- Money is not medicine but it purchases medicine for health.

- What's wrong with his masculinity, other than his name only.

- Art it is the concrete shape that thought took.

- Arm wrestling with the Lord is vain you can't win.

- Now that all newspapers write the same thing, then there is no need to read them all separately.

- The one who comes and goes is not the same as the one who died and got lost are not the same.

- That is not fair to say we won't trust anyone in life instead say we will know who to trust.

- Open your wound inside only to the creator with low sound. He will haer you, no doubt.

- The same day may be a scream for some, a wedding for some others.

- Among us there are those who are like fire balls,they burns those they touch and also to those who touch them burns.

- If you say the world is narrow, do not be afraid there is God above.

- In some families a saint and maid are together.

- The fruit tree shows its talent in the spring and give fruit in summer.

- The future scares some, excites other men.

- I know where to be stupid and where stupid to be found.

- Be careful, we are just passing through this world on the contrary we are passing through ourselves.

- One's own expectations in this life tires him the most.

- Now, I'm an expatriate myself, it is a so long excile that upsets.

- There is lust in the way men look at women, there's jealousy in the way a woman looks at a woman.

- The most orphan of the family is the father, and then mother comes.

- If you speak to people more then you will not be understood. If you talk to people taller than their heights, you become incomprehensible.

- Now old days are behind my back, I laugh at them though I'm sad.

- If his mother hadn't died, he would have cried a lot these days due to the dire situation of her son.

- Without exception every life is pregnant with death.

- Now making crying is free, however, crying is prohibited.

- When they grow up even small fish open up to the oceans as the seas are narrow for them.

- Our originals were soil, our bottom is soil, and our top will be covered with soil, too.

- The devil fills an empty gun. the enemy fills an empty brain.

- Those with crazy nerves have no boundaries.

- You left me your shadow, however, I left glory to you to borrow.

- Some rot from work, some rot inside from the thought.

- I don't have a little tongue, because of what I've been through shocks, I swallowed it.

- Some shed tears, some also make it shed with fears.

- A young girl is like a luxury outfit in a window, she should not lower her value of herself.

- Providing that he is cruel, his son is his seed after all.

- We love some people so much that even if they die, they always stay fresh in memories.

- Now that we're going to be broken so let's break with laughter.

- Either you speak loudly or you whisper the same for the deaf.

- Someone who finds his cat in each song means he has lost a lot.

- Providing you're out of charge, don't push your luck much.

- Blind people look at a person through their own mirror of the heart.

- If you are being pointed with a finger. You are guilty or too strong or either .

- The unchecked true information brought by the liar doesn't go beyond sensation.

- Someone who became to you a goat, innately you will become his shepherd.

- The burden of the body is carried by heart the fatigue of heart is because of this.

- My life is not diminishing, the days I will meet Him are getting lesser.

- All poets are peasants of the same village also travelers of the same road.

- Even if you stand low, don't sit with the low in character.

- If he doesn't talk, he holds a grudge, if he talks, who will prevent him from punch.

- Reverse gear does not work in laws for flaws .

- OK! This world is a lie but not an ordinary lie.

- Man shows his true face and essence when he is in hard trouble.

- Time, devalues everything over time.

- The reasons are false, but it's always the same Person who does.

- Live in line with your money, do not live according to your air, Honey.

- Too much sacrifice, that is, more than enough leads to much disloyalty.

- Our origin is soil, maybe because of that some among us are really mud.

- Every creature has a concern of reproduction, either from the root, or from the male.

- On purpose some people prefer solitude to be happy.

- Twice a year we celebrate the holiday with the mad.

- Anyone who is not able to compete is crushed by the opponent disgracefully.

- Sometimes we ask what our friends don't have; such us, understanding, sacrifice. We get angry when they don't give as a result.

- If you want everyone to understand you, you will speak the language that everyone understands.

- Whatever you push for it to happen, in case it happens, that's a victory.

- Only the, pirate literati practice their profession behind toilet doors.

- I just feel like leaving this place only because of someone.

- As others lose, the goods in our hands gain more value in our eyes.

- Blessing and goodwill travel together side by side.

- People are blind to the mistakes of the most loved one, but the thorn of them sinks deeper.

- Let's be frank, but not obscene as a young.

- The master talks through his art, valiant talks with his horse.

- Wounds that do not heal will hurt you very deeply.

- With a smile on the face, a person becomes beautiful without make-up.

- People don't need conflict, they must be closer to each other more frequent.

- Nowadays, everyone is talking and eating out of their own smart pocket.

- Sword blow cuts people, whip blow sets them in motion.

- Character in man is above all abilities.

- We've made a habit of being deceived. That's why we're always being cheated on.

- Yours, not even double standards, but out of standards.

- The person who admits that he is ignorant in fact, he's a real intellectual.

- You were my only thing earlier but now you have become my everything.

- Some people twist so fast that they even make us dizzy.

- The donkey's leadership is till the caravan turns upside down.

- And the roar of the lion is lion-like again.

- Snakes always use their fork when they eat their food.

- A person needs a face to laugh and an eye to cry.

- Right now, you have to say yes or no. –Thus, I say Yes or No.

- Those who are not interested are also not informed, too.

- Mud like dough is not a blessing without being cooked.

- Someone standing in his place without moving forward, actually he counts from behind.

- Behave as if you're at the tip of the barrel you must always be vigilant.

- Not too silence but very harmonic loudness is desirable.

- If you're temporary, you can't be selective; in case you're selective, you're permanent.

- Providing you start rendering of account on the ground, you'll be comfortable under it.

- You write the past but you cannot live the past.

- Pay attention to your heart while walking, and your mold while sitting.

- Since you cannot fall in love, absolutely spouse must have fallen in love with you.

- Keep the rope of your soul short and the rope of your dreams long.

- Allah does not hasten, because all time is His.

- The one who lost his way is actually lost himself, not his way.

- Provided that you work with pleasure like a bee, you will give precious products like honey.

- He who gives the bad news like good news is not your friend.

- Each person has a personal region and a shadow. However, his value depends on his manners.

- The heart also breaks, but quietly and in its own way.

- Those who do not see also see; such as, nightmares or dreams.

- But those who are dealing with meaningful things are understood even through feelings.

- If we believe in the power of love as much as we believe in violence, all matters will be resolved.

- Being a widow in the country is being a glassless window.

- Their hostility to us is either because of their religion or because of our region.

- You choose to be something, we choose to die for one thing.

- Everyone wants to own the found diamond.

- He's throwing character, take a little bit for you, too.

- A failed wise is prefferable than a successful fool.

- Satan does not only interfere with tea and soup, but also with the brutal and the persecutor.

- My goat's world is the world of livelihood.

- Justice is blind, but her hands are very sensitive.

- The borders drawn with a ruler are much more hurtful than those drawn with a pen.

- From five million kilometers away, the world is like a speck of dust. It really does not matter for some.

- I'm not leaving you to death, I'm leaving you to return with health.

- Disasters come in loud, the trick is to notice them.

- The peak at which the tyrant reached is the just beginning of his end.

- If you find your worth in life, whatever you do for it is still less.

- If you believe in the power of prayer, a door to the sky opens even if you're at the bottom of the well.

- Be the flare for those who love you.

- My future is uncertain, but I will definitely reach it.

- The characters of the people are hidden in their laughter.

- Don't rely on common crowds; the day comes when those who come behind you run behind you.

- Something that Satan makes you small, goes its root till the hell.

- A man of the hand prefers someone who plays very well, not someone who plays a lot.

- No one willingly fall into mud.

- On arrival, they welcomed with drum and greeted with drill and on the way back, only the harmonica was played.

- Everything that starts, ends one day, but love pain is exception.

- You know once you were small, your dad knows you all well.

- The one with the head down usually has a broken heart.

- Lying is not a character, but a weakness of character.

- His attitude towards me was so cold that I thought winter has come again.

- Selfishness makes you lonely; though egoists don't die of loneliness, but they die alone.

- Only those whose excuse is over say 'for aught I care!'

- The season on the balcony and the season on the roof do not match each other.

- Roses bloomed in your garden, so did they on your face.

- Anyone who opens their eyes wide won't cause any trouble even in fight.

- Don't always remain as an audience, even if you're an audience.

- Whilst there are people everywhere, but there is no humanity everywhere.

- The pages of the book are odd and even; I feel sorry for odd ones.

- The lover is like a headache; she doesn't come to neglect.

- Do not compromise your dignity or else you become an appetizer for malevolent people.

- Look at the luck in the woman, she found a house.

- Listen and learn, thus, both win and earn.

- He who lies to save his life is more innocent than he who lies to save the moment.

- Pigeons fly in flocks, swans fly with only one not in mobs.

- A positive development must be an honorable enhancement.

- The regenerators finally get the undefeated title.

- If sleep is half death, I wish death was so sweet.

- The one who makes the sacrifice takes real pleasure mode than interlocutor.

- Most people wear masks out of recognition, not from embarrassment.

- The rear tires follow the front ones, but under one condition, if they go straight.

- A drop of tears has a flood of emotions much more than wetness.

- Maybe interlocutor's clothes get dirty but mud thrower's hands also gets dirty.

- The sun rises again from where it sets, in fact no disappearance.

- Trust is like a timid gazelle; it runs away with the slightest suspicion and disappears.

- Some in this world win by proximity of blood and some others by height and handset.

- The owner of sin asks forgiveness from the owner of the day; from Goodness.

- Don't say who died because of a lie; Is there anyone who doesn't die?

- Your hands have lines unlike mine, but my face has embarrassment to shame.

- If you shrink your mouth, you won't upset anyone.

- Anyone who goes crazy is put in hospital, that is easy.

- Look after your lady like your eyes or else you will be blind.

- You don't lose from mistakes, but on one condition, if you record the massage it.

- The price of a clean conscience is a lifetime of sacrifice.

- Tearful, young people make a mess of me, very fearful.

- If I love, my heart will stand, or else I will die.

- Excuse; just a nice mint to use.

- Anyone who looks for shame does more shame.

- Success is very proud; it doesn't come to your feet, you ought to go.

- Providing his essence is not inclined, his eye does not watch it.

- In this Life, some lose out of type and some lose downright.

- Crime is like a detective; it follows you for life.

- The beginning of the savings is **uuf** and the end **ooh**.

- The reputation of the good is heard, so the tyrant's end, too.

- Don't say too heavy; lift it slowly.

- Snow falls on the homes of the poor but it falls on the dreams of the rich.

- Be a monkey, rather than being a beast.

- Don't say I'm leaving, your shadow denies you, in vain.

- There would be no loyalty to the crippled horse.

- Even if the smarties change sides in their mission, they continue doing their job. This is a character in them.

- If you became an ass, rider would be found.

- One who fights for his honor, defeats the one who fights for his own benefit.

- Although his work is dirty, his earnings are clean.

- Dexterity is not deceiving, it's about eliminating obstacles.

- I am strong enough not to think that I am weak.

- It was very plain, but not a simple plan.

- There is no cruelty in justice and there is no justice in cruelty.

- The most effective life lesson is the lesson drawn from mistakes you experienced.

- Not summer but winter is the winner of all seasons.

- We really experience the winter: both inside and outside.

- Art is the most concrete form of reflection of the inner senses of the human being.

- If winter is the end of everything, spring that comes right after it is a new beginning.

- A way to meet a dead hero is to die in his way.

- He's head-legged; he's always thinking about his interests and chases them.

- In the past, we used to go to where the world goes. Nowadays we're doing the opposite.

- We didn't run out of, the very opposite we were scattered to grow.

- By going the wrong way, you don't get to the right place.

- The burden of truth is heavy, not every conscience can bear it.

- The feeling of belonging and owning finds its real meaning in an ideal couple.

- When there is a barcode on your lips, your age is obvious.

- We take our strength not from the armor, but from the inscription in our forehead.

- The mountain is a lot until you pass over and then it seems nothing after you passed.

- The pain of the person whose tongue is burnt passes but never the one whose mouth was burned passes.

- The spoils of war cover up the strangeness of war.

- The children of the palace cannot understand the children of poor place.

- The elephant meddle their noses everywhere.

- This world is full of people who say this world is mine, and cemeteries are full of such people who thought that was in wain.

- It doesn't matter whether the stone of the river or the poor's tear.

- He's not a relative but a real vulture in active.

- In the eye of mine past is nothing, however, the future is hammer power like thing.

- Yet she wasn't a magician, she charmed me.

- Ice, as a word, is repulsive in winter and attractive in summer.

- The names of idiots are given so as not to confuse them. As for the smart, they do not need to, they already reveal themselves.

- From every calamity a lesson to take arises.

- Father's money, mother's prayer is appreciated.

- The flower that miscalculates the spring will fade before it blooms.

- A quarter friends leave everything in words; they don't act.

- Even in the most difficult times, falling into pessimism is a weakness of faith.

- Some people die of pain, others die of starvation.

- Maybe you can make beautiful shapes but you cannot turn silver into gold by beating.

- Don't let the devil find out that you hurry.

- The only behavior that the dishonorable cannot do is an honorable stance.

- Do not go with the speed of a snake, go like a bird flying.

- He was born hard, what's more, his shape was weird.

- My Lord is your Lord too, but what you worship is not mine.

- A calamity becomes lighter in general sense and becomes more intense in private.

- The good inspire you, the bad do not even greet, too.

- I've seen sensitive valiant men who don't even step on lady's foot print.

- If you're claiming to be going right, turn around and look for your foot track.

- Lazy speaks with his chin, hardworking talks with his hand.

- To cross the mountain, first of all, you have to be alive.

- Money shows its strength when you have at present and makes its value felt when it is absent.

- The knowledge gained from one's own experience is more valuable than the knowledge acquired through reading.

- Just as judges are the common conscience of society, scholars are also common wisdom.

- The hopes of the future erase the sediment of the past.

- There is such a thing called justice, but it does not exist everywhere.

- Instead of being a hand to hold, be a fruit branch to hold.

- Archives are the certificate of the innocent and the death sentence of criminals.

- In failure we generally blame anyone else for making effort less.

- A man's price is as much as what he deigns.

- The tongue lies but eyes do not confirm it.

- Liars convince so quickly but they are very difficult to convince.

- His relationship to reality is that he's just living.

- There is a connection between the dog and the repulsiveness, the patch and the sewer.

- Socks and gloves are different. The glove is fixed, although you can wear socks either way.

- I'm fickle about throwing away my tittle.

- For mistakes behave badly to yourself, however, be like a teacher to the poor.

- Snowflakes do not get you as wet as raindrops, but they're rather serious.

- He scattered himself when he thought he was going to distribute smiles.

- Completing this day safely is not the guarantee of tomorrow.

- Conscience endures all kinds of pain, but it can't handle injustice as big as hair.

- Some arrive at the destination crushing, some arrive at the target by digging, but no one arrives by traveling.

- If he is underfoot, there is no point in being any longer proud.

- The effect of lies manifests itself as bruises on some faces and redness on others.

- We talked about our bright future in the dark.

- Those who speak with behavior put on tour those who just speak with words.

- As time passes over us, it picks up the hair, rubs and wrinkles the faces.

- Do not forget that you are human and that your enemy is a human, don't break his honor.

- Hand washes the other hand, eyes see what other eye sees

- The minda, eyes and ears of fools are on their lips.

- What man always thinks and says is not the same, they can be reflected in different fame.

- Gulls also make victory signs, but not with a hand, but with their tails.

- If you don't like someone, pour sauce over him.

- Do not beg for mercy from an unscrupulous one; If he had had, he would have used it anyway.

- People see through eyes but keep what they see in their hearts.

- However, those who look at themselves from the ground zero feel the value of others.

- If the master of the house is a woman, the lord of the house behaves like a cat at home.

- Yesterday is so clear and tomorrow is flu for everyone even for you.

- No one can impose on me without Allah creating a reason.

- Against poor-quality people, the character of bitch people speaks.

- You come across good people either in heaven or in the cemetery.

- Confirm the case, but don't give birth to a lie while reporting the incident.

- Even if you sleep in the same place, you cannot have the same dream.

- Where do I find you?-He said, 'I have not lost'.

- The one whom my Lord calls my servant we should love him the best.

- Courage can only achieve its goal if it is supported by reason.

- In some parts of the world some are moving at the speed of donkey and some are moving at the speed of light.

- He didn't have so much fun, he never married even one.

- Their looks may deceive you, but, negroes' bones are also white.

- I don't know about Kaf mountain, but there are many giants in history.

- A poor person lives inside everyone; he comes into existance in bad moments.

- The clouds became more and more black with anger and eventually exploded.

- You're fighting the enemy; not his honor, watch out!

- Fake friends rejoice at your failure ad will be so sorry for your success.

- Those who know no boundaries in friendship, they cannot draw the boundaries of hostility.

- A person must be either a teacher or a student; the teacher of past and the student of future.

- Everyone wonders your debt, not your zodiac sign in fact.

- In life, not the one who has the most things but the one who knows how to settle for less is happier.

- Instead of consulting a negative person, go and talk to a bagger's son.

- I say hold then understood the bold.

- I read what the man wrote, but I could not learn even a word.

- Bread at home is sweeter than pastry in the neighbor.

- A mother knows who she gives birth to, a neighbor knows who she feeds.

- Bee offers honey to his friend and poison to the enemy.

- The devil's collaborator in man is the soul.

- Satan is man's worst enemy; you contrasts with the natural character when you get along with it.

- The descent road takes its revenge on the ramp on the turn.

- The difference between nylon and gold can only be seen in the face of fire.

- Those who made several mistakes in the past are hard to deceive.

- The enemy gets a terrible pleasure from the beating of two cronies with each other.

- You can't ask anyone his name but you can ask anyone the address.

- Those who take their steps with thought, make few mistakes, even if they do not see ahead.

- Everyone has a father but two grandfathers.

- Comfort gives rest to some and turns others away from religion fast.

- A harsh winter makes the homeless cry, but then the rivers cascade high.

- Like parents, teachers also misjudges their students. In their eyes, they never grow up.

- He is so jealous that he has no tolerance even towards his shadow.

- The grim reaper continues to take lives, yet persecution does not continue.

- Be a wanted element, not an intermediate element.

- May Allah live by the smell of a son, not by the fear of a son.

- There are many Iam fond of but I don't have a girlfriend.

- They asked a fat person do you go with your belly everywhere, isn't it difficult, and he said yes, but he goes before me.

- His liver is in his mouth, everyone thinks he's liverless.

- I like oil, I do not enjoy greasers, at all.

- Older people do not rely on technology as much as young people do.

- Believe or not that python is exactly a ton.

- Although that is additional revenue for some, this sum is his only income.

- Normally, meat is not crushed, but the one in human is excluded.

- Accuracy is an extension of the child character.

- These are eared but they do not feel the right of servants earned.

- Nature does not accept emptiness; even wind fills an empty daire.

- And he who prays makes the prayer one of the righteous ways.

- We're gonna make it, not by pushing but by hugging.

- People who are hungry for knowledge never fill their saddlebags.

- Pity for the needy, but never for yourself I don't mean your ID.

- Those who do not compromise their pleasure are forced to be self-sacrificing.

- We're like months neighboring months with you, side by side, but there's a year difference between us.

- Recommending is also considered a kind of supplement.

- Inside love spills out of the tongue and appears on the face.

- Try not to be a hellish passion, however, to be an heir to heaven.

- The most loving one is a mother's heart, she's so kind and smart.

- All the new cars have the same story, whereas each of the old ones has its own story.

- Not everything happens as you say but it happens in His own way.

- History also writes the wrong right.

- Even if you're a scholar, in case you say you don't know, an ignoramus'll make you look like himself.

- Allah overwhelms, but He also does not put desperate opening new doors.

- Every month, every day, even every minute, doesn't pass without coming by to me.

- In the tears of others, maybe you can float your ship, but you can't stop it from sinking.

- The only thing a person can't prevent is not tears, but his aging fears.

- An angry man knows where to start, but he doesn't gues where to stop.

- Even if it moves, a shadow is a shadow, not the real one.

- The man of solution and the man of the revolution aren't supposed to be face to face, but they should be shoulder to shoulder.

- It is mentality rather than property that develops nations.

- The tongue has no bones if the bone had had a tongue I wonder what he would have said.

- I looked at your picture, I couldn't count how many faces you had.

- Step in the direction you're going, do not do it for place you're looking.

- Those who clean one place and dirty another are not considered clean.

- Those who say that they will jump the age are jumped on the knife unknowingly.

- The dog's barking into the darkness is not to scare anybody, but because of its own fear.

- Human quality is revealed not by how he treats his relatives, but by how he treats the strangers.

- You cannot keep owning commodities without perceiving intelligent duties.

- Those who know the value of blessing best are those who economize at the maximum level.

- God! Either bring his end or end his lineage or death.

- Don't be arrogant, look at the grave; an inevitable end.

- Although the guilty prisoner and the innocent inmate stay in the same cell, their torment is not at the same level.

- Friend completes the deficiency of a friend again.

- Ignorance catches the one who breaks away from knowledge.

- Devil's toy is not just beaches, but all people with multiple faces.

- A person who passes out won't get anywhere, either west or south.

- Don't look for the peace you've lost at home in the street, look for it where you lost.

- You say, grandchild, we say the seed that will grow as a spike.

- If you don't want to brood, you will think before you decide.

- Our biggest weapon is our righteousness written pen.

- The one who loses his excitement is close to lose his life, I put my signment.

- However, wherever a man knows being a man, then the woman remembers being a woman.

- Anyone with arms open in fact, he has opened the door of his heart beforehand.

- I intended to call you human, but my tongue doesn't allow me to say it.

- If you give the devil a place as big as a pinhole, he will expand it to become blind well.

- If you go back in time, your good deeds shine like a lamp, while evil ones seem like a lake of pitch.

- The things that we want to say are shaped in our hearts are poured out from our tongue.

- Seeking someone's loss must be considered loyalty to it.

- The wolf's persistence in hunting is more of hunger drive than its perseverance.

- What would happen if he offered you sherbet when his hands were dirty?

- To appreciate heroism is also another heroism.

- The groom either forgot the word or swallowed it.

- There is no imitation of heroism, there is an appreciation.

- Always keep your direction towards the world, and keep another eye on the afterlife.

- The obstacles in front of you seem big, but those remained behind seem trivial.

- The armchair does not increase the value of a man but measures.

- Man mingles with man but man does not interfere with man.

- There are those who live without gratitude enough to dig their own grave.

- Smart people learn the right lesson from the curved one.

- Do not leave your Lord, leave the consequences to your Lord.

- Grief meets the losers also fate comforts them.

- Fulfilling dreams is not just a job of strength, it's a job of perseverance.

- Ladies raise their eyebrows when asked their age.

- The one who comes with a crush goes with the punishment

- May Allah put you so high that no one can belittle you.

- Hold your chin before you go against him.

- Someone who is in trouble sounds like his head is in the toilet, It's very probable.

- A liar tries to convince someone else that he doesn't believe himself.

- As soon as he became president he changed himself before changing anything.

- Some with their beauties affects their addressees some with of their features.

- I seek refuge in the forgiveness of my Lord, not the mercy of the wrongdoer court.

- Some of us get the disease, some of us make invitation for this.

- No one could say that his conscience was atrophied; what is not used does not become blunt.

- Although the trees bloom in their seasons, the face of an optimist one has no season, it is always in bloom.

- There is no such a thing as luck. Luck only preparation for a probable opportunity.

- In appearance, he's man-like, but, in fact he's not a man so tight.

- Whether a person lived or not can be found out from the traces he left.

- Tears of joy contain more emotion than pain.

- Those who want to do evil use the weaknesses of human beings.

- A mermaid doesn't look like a maid.

- Until now, the property of anyone sharing on facebook has not diminished.

- You'll treat everyone according to their level, but not for those who have no level.

- Tell me not the pain of separation, but talk about the pleasure of reunion.

- Friends are as like sidewalks; Although there is no organic bond between you and them, you get the feeling of security from them.

- If you ask someone for something he doesn't have you will be disappointed. Such as, honour, humanity, and so on.

- Among friends don't be a game breaker, be a game maker.

- How did you make it so big inside; baby born at 5 kilos.

- The great sun goes down, how do these ships float without going down.

- A fake friend's friendship is fake but his hostility is real.

- He who is respectful to everybody does not need to be anxious.

- Even if he's a good friend of him, won't be a brother to him.

- An unfair person is expected to be mean.

- As brother I stepped in my bosom, but you came out the black stone.

- Melt away for me, even get lost by melting inside me.

- Who can say that the one who throws the rod is the same as the one who pace at the seaside.

- Anything new is spoken in the language first, but then the hands complete what it said.

- The dress you wear not only makes the exterior beautiful, it also enhances the interior.

- Although the hunter can do his job with one eye, he still needs two eyes.

- Lack of knowledge makes courage, flattery enslaves people.

- Whether the wheel goes fast or slow, it takes the same way. By the way, if it goes fast, it shortens the duration.

- The ears, the eyes nourish the soul; the mouth nourish the stomach.

- Skullcap covers bald, make-up covers the freckles.

- Regardless of its level, one's words don't touch so heavily to himself.

- Even though the cheeky adds her honor to her bread, he never gets full.

- Being honorable of the enemy is more important than honority of your friend.

- I'd rather be misunderstood than I'd rather be misrepresented.

- Anyone who wrestles with a lion must have claws like a lion.

- God, help those who burn a lot, not those who lie inside.

- Some kill time, some kill each other. As a result they are killers.

- A person character changes when he believes or gets hurt.

- The heart can't stand sadness, so too, the shovel can't stand the barn.

- The most honest behavior expected from a liar is to speak of his open identity.

- But good, but bad, each is the art of God.

- Nobody dies for anyone, nor does he laugh.

- The sea embraces what is inside and threatens what is on the shore.

- Yesterday is compensated by taking lessons, tomorrow's supply is possible as of today.

- If you've taken the wrong path, the faulty is not the road. Because every road leads somewhere.

- A mother carries her child into the future in her heart and on her lap.

- Once the devil get to know this guy, he'll have to reset himself.

- Don't be fooled by appearances; there is God in the essence of everything.

- The shoe shows its quality in snow and heroic characters also show their quality in the row.

- Even in the most difficult situation, there is an opportunity to save one's honor.

- All roads are open; some lead to trouble and some to The God.

- Even if animals don't know how to cry, they make us cry though.

- The difference between a rooster and a clock is that one bells when it's set up, the other bells without setting up.

- When every creature is viewed with the eyes of wisdom, God appears.

- Someone who is a devil inside is not complete in his image.

- This is not only a matter of Ahmet, Mehmet, But both Ahmet's and Mehmet's matter, of course.

- Life is a one-man game; everyone is playing their parts, almost the same..

- Each life is a separate excitement unique to its owner .

- In togetherness nightingale with rose, lucky one is the rose, the unfortunate is the nightingale.

- Good and evil are the rings of a chain; the one who holds one reaches its continuation.

- Whoever roars like a lion must have a heart like it.

- Those who grow old together don't realize that they're getting old.

- The good can get along well with everyone, and the bad can get along with neither the good nor the bad.

- If you were coming late, at least come swinging not by shaking.

- As a rule; the lover's face is cheeky and the master's eye is a thief.

- Those who loves someone so much, and those who hates someone are both blind. The former blind from extreme sentimentality, and the latter is blind because of ingratitude.

- What we think and what we make impressiom on someone else is different.

- What I have is not spring fever, but morning sleepiness.

- I say neither the first step nor the last step; I say step by step forward instead.

- What you don't like about someone is that what you cannot adopt.

- Anybody whom you don't give your lice you can't trust your dog.

- Many chickens appreciate roosters, and many buildings appreciate debris are valued.

- A self-helpless one incites the vices of the evil.

- The good advice should be said to the one who understands, otherwise it will be wasted.

- In general, we hurry into the toilet like a passenger, come out like a criminal.

- Children have made the biggest progress in the family today. While they used to be the guests of the house, now they are the head of the family.

- Whoever crosses the ocean does not drown in the stream.

- The thorn of the rose is endured for the sake of the beauty of rose.

- There is a dignity in what is original.

- There is bondage in interest and courage in righteousness.

- Women not only stole men's hearts, but also confiscated their clothes partly.

- Those who have nothing to give people so they hurt people.

- Bar none, each lifetime has an expiration date.

- The eye cannot see the other eye, but one sees what the other sees.

- Even if every person can be wrong, but not every person misleads you.

- Peace does not come alone, it definitely brings something with it.

- The dream land where you can't reach, you can dream about it like rich.

- The one who can't stand up straight, his shadow is crooked.

- The one whose heart is rock, don't doubt that his yeast is from mud.

- When young, you work for living, in old age you try to live.

- The war is won with arms, however, the peace is maintained with love.

- If you have a lot of memories, you're not rich, you're old.

- We did not have memories together with you, let's combine our dreams with each other.

- If love isn't real, then what was I going through?

- It cannot be the nightingale that placed on the shoulder of the poor, it must be an owl.

- He got so in the air that he would almost fly if he wasn't lame.

- If he's arrogant, he's not worth making friends.

- His dissatisfaction is not because of your name, but inasmuch as his own blood.

- Sometimes it happens that a person determines his life line with his intuition.

- Some people are created to lean on, some are to endure.

- Her husband is a counselor, but mine is a sailor.

- Every rooster chirps in its own dumpster, every dog barks in front of its owner's house.

- The inside of the heart is about the owner, and the outside is about those who need compassion.

- Man's opponent is the better, his enemy is the bad.

- Do not follow the advice of the enemy unless you have checked with your friend's recommendation.

- A cunning person does every job, a smart person does a job very well.

- Your enemy is a thorn in your eye, your friend is a shroud to your dead body.

- Every season has a beginning and an the end, but with the exception of winter.

- The ferocity of the thorn contributes beauty to the rose.

- Darkness swallows objects which are without light, even mountains, and the light makes them vomit that darkness swallowed.

- A fake friend escorts you till the door, a real friend escorts until you crosses the hill.

- Use your image in friendship, use your speed in peace.

- The only thing we want to delay but cannot extend is the time of death.

- Misdemeanor is a kind of tear that does not hold a patch.

- Even if disaster foretells its coming, a thief doesn't.

- The extreme proportion of modesty is understood as helplessness by the ignorant.

- Even though your death is not the end of this world, but that is the end of your world.

- Sometimes a pet that you raise with your own hand will enslave you.

- Every new stuff gets old, including even every part of human body.

- False friends are like wax; they can never stand the heat.

- Even though the heart is fake it's full of facts.

- If you read the book backward, he should understand correctly in a single word.

- A brain controls the woman, and also she controls her husband, though he's a man.

- The brave equates with foolishness if he shows off his courage at every opportunity.

- Imprudence is the secret invitation of the accident.

- It is funny to ask for a wonderful view and give less money.

- I wish everyone was as innocent as they say.

- Peace at home reflects out as beauties.

- Those who are light themselves do not mind the darkness.

- Not his enemy but his friend misleads a person many.

- Anyone who doesn't appreciate today never knows tomorrow's value. Because if today is gold tomorrow is silver.

- The world is a lie without fail, but what experiences we go through in it is real.

- Some are earning the living from dough and some are from mud though.

- Every road has a walker, every goer has a reason.

- If the wicked's mentor is the devil, the devil's greatest perpetrator is the tyrant.

- The room of those whose ceiling is sky their room is as wide as the earth surface.

- Animals don't have an insured job, but they never worry about the future.

- Each person has a raw state and complete fate.

- She made his most devoted lover his most faithful slave. So she became the wife of the slave, in a way.

- She is so sensitive that if someone blows her nose near her, she immediately catches a cold.

- Every road is for Allah, whoever sets out will reach Him, lonely or as a team.

- In order not to be afraid of hell, you're not in need of courage but worship.

- He's so angry; whoever's bothering him, he puts a bullet in.

- Those who do not keep their words cannot keep their places.

- Those who is failure to pull you are surely weaker than you.

- My father always wanted me to be like himself, and I wanted to be myself. In the end, neither of both had happened.

- A man belongs to a place where he finds peace.

- If the world is so ugly why are there so many bidders?

- One victim, the other volunteer victim to him.

- When young, you make films, when we're old, you make health film in hospital.

- The persecution is not the end even the bottom has been seen.

- Any of us in life only plays what's written for ourselves beforehand.

- How a person lives is as an important clueas how he'll die.

- For those who can't read time well, time comes and they make read it him.

- There is a lot of demand for love, but very few people can feed and raise it in their bosom.

- The dream of a silk worm is to knit for itself a cocoon.

- Man is the child of the environment in which he lives.

- Happiness is the dream of people of all ages.

- Lawlessness reached its peak, now it's time to build its walls.

- The order is bad for some, very okay for some men.

- Do not mistreat the person made a mistake by giving him a second punishment. Otherwise, you will also make a mistake.

- The road is clear, you can go on your way, dear.

- Every beauty has a buyer absolutely.

- The door that opens from the hearts of mother extends to heaven one way or the other.

- Speaking is an art; its bricks are the words we use.

- Decays are not rotten again, as they rot from the inside out.

- That's better not to view than to watch bad scenery.

- Those who make a habit of destroying don't have time to repair it.

- First a showdown with yourself sins then the purification comes.

- An orphan's property is poisonous; eaten but it is not digestible.

- Don't say love until you're full; If you love, you can't get enough.

- Although he wants to be a victim to me human beings are not sacrificed.

- In destiny, though there is grief, there is no compulsion, in brief.

- The value of Zero comes from ignoring itself not because it counted itself too much.

- Every event has to have a reason, each person has to have a plausible reason.

- He who steals from the night gives it back from the daytime.

- Let's not throw men, let's step up to win them.

- Some people supply their needs from the street, some from the bazaar in deed.

- Those who do not settle for less he'll waste when he finds a lot.

- The problem you've got fid of is no longer your problem.

- The oppressed is also predatory; he tears himself up.

- Some come and leave a trail, some go away and leave gossip.

- Some of your friends are ordinary, some are complete men literally.

- If you give someone less, he'll be cheeky, if you don't give any, he'll be shameless.

- In case you don't act the way others want, they think you were transfigured.

- Mothers cry a lot, especially that of those who do not know how to get away with.

- You cannot anticipate his expectation, nor can you satisfy him. This is certain.

- if someone claims that there is no possibility of doing wrong, as a result he may becomes a victim of possibility.

- Those who know their ancestors well, stay away from mistakes.

- Lazy people leave problems to the youngsters, but hardworking one leave prosperity to sons and daughters.

- What really occupies the mind is not what we say but those which we can't say.

- He who does not calculate the result of his action can challenge even the world.

- Life tells his lesson in the shortest way in a practical way.

- The person whose capital is a lie will not run out of property but his property will be plundered.

- In order to desire perfection one has to be perfect.

- He who intent to go, only hopes, however, if he realises it he gets.

- Ingenuity is to understand your fake friend before deceiving you; after being deceived, everyone can find out it.

- Every look has value in the human evil eye.

- Beards constantly grow, even touch the ground, but will discolor over time.

- Hunger is a side character of second-degree people; they never get enough.

- The man of the case is also the cure man.

- Man's soft belly is his family, but his softest place is his only child.

- The seasons have changed, yet the climate has not changed.

- Everyone smiles when they hear the word life, but when they say death, they suddenly get serious.

- Abundance rain is only fertile to the cultivated field.

- If you treat a mother like an old woman, she will come out of motherhood, becomes a stranger.

- Hunger for knowledge is like quenching thirst with seawater; the more you drink, the more thirsty you become.

- A person's brain and waist thicken when they are not used.

- Marriage is the art of turning fairy tales into stories.

- Some slopes are not felt until they are crossed.

- The steps of the ladder of success are made of the substance of patience.

- Although the camel is crooked everywhere, the path it goes is straight.

- Don't call him just a child, he's your past symbol.

- The old wolf is caught with new traps.

- Not the one who makes peace with the devil but those who fights the devil, wins.

- Since you love money so much, keep your name, let's change your surname with it.

- Keep an eye on your work, not someone else's food.

- I say to those who ask whether the uninspired bread can be eaten without any additives,

I respond, thank God I add to it and eat peacefully.

- Loving is one thing, Love is everything.

- When God's mercy rains in a downpour, what is the use of an umbrella?

- The tiger walks, whereas the turtle migrates wherever it goes.

- Do not pass by saying the metrobus, jump right up at once.

- Excessive mind tires the person.

- Resentment is the precursor outburst of anger.

- Every person has an uninhabited syndrome.

- The bottom of someone is visible in a sentence he produced, but some are like the bottomless well below.

- Anyone who says I will make no mistakes, he makes the mistake right before starting.

- A mandatory living persons are troublesome living people.

- Everyone has a story; some can't end by telling, some others swallow and cannot bring the words end.

- He who eats at someone's table without merit, eats out of his honor.

- Ramadan is not a burden for a Muslim, but It is a very valuable domain.

- I 'm not fond of anything about him other than his name.

- There is an am for the chicken to lie down. What about you?

- There is no end to evil, but the branches of goodness extend up to the heaven.

- When those who do not want freedom of thought, they want it after they fell.

- If you really want to see that you're not perfect, take a look at your past.

- If our denominator is right, our share will be neat.

- Some of us are being tested with the siblings yet the others are tested with other things.

- Life loves the persistent ones, not the hashish. While he is very stingy with the former, he officially presents himself to the latter.

- Don't forget the traffic sign, even if you go straight.

- If the good are the spectators, the bad ones will be actual.

- Sometimes I complain about myself to myself.

- The friendship of those who care about you is extremely valuable.

- You look for your lost where you fell, but you look for someone you lost and couln't find in the cemetery.

- Everyone tries to ride the low donkey.

- Realism doesn't taste good unless we add a little romance sauce.

- The golden key is more ingenious than the lockpick.

- A fool doesn't learn much from a smart man, however, the smart learn a lot from an idiot.

- If you plant seeds, the grain grows, it's not like that in friendship if you cheat on your friend, everything will be all over.

- Even if a person who does work can make a mistake, the person who does not work does a lot more mistakes.

- Although it's up to you to ride a horny horse, it will not your decision where to get off.

- Alm protects the giver and feeds the one who accepts it.

- Listen, my two eyes ! Where are there pear without stemless or garbage-free grapes.

- The only thing that can't be bought with money is humanity.

- As the world is a lie in essence anyone who comes, and then goes so becomes a lie.

- The name of the soup has changed, the taste of it has changed.

- Art thrives only in a peaceful environment.

- Who does not think of tomorrow loses both today and tomorrow.

- Anything except justice is expected from tyrant.

- No one is alone; at least he ows a loyal shadow.

- The mountains frighten those who look at it from afar yet embraces the one who walks on it.

- All that a person does in life consists of using the means provided by The Lord.

- Don't step on the wet thing, step on the stone, think!

- A goden word to you! Not all tempting words are true.

- Every mistake made by the wise honors the fool.

- The one who derails will drown in the rivers.

- A gaze does not pass tangent, it necessarily touches and goes.

- Suppose that very closest relative of you has died, you know but you can't believe, thus, knowing is different from believing.

- The one who flies in the air and the one on the ground does not fall with the same force; one crashes to the ground, the other just hangs.

- You cannot have someone dance in a bad mood even if you play the most playful song.

- The kindness of some people is just until they get behind the wheel.

- Do not look at the forbidden goods, Look at the holly books.

- You're complaining about getting old. There's only one way to stop, however, it it doesn't work for you either.

- The knot of fate cannot be dissolved before it's time comes.

- Time is the most reliable witness that gives the best answers to questions and problems.

- A person becomes happy by by rebuilding, but not by breaking

- Without exception everyone has expectations from time.

- Shadow is the Negro appearance of its owner

- Who says summer is the season; it's just a long day. As for spring it is a shortest season that ends in the blink of an eye.

- The ground is a refuge for those who die, who falls, or even who feel ashamed.

- The gesture against the gesture makes one feel better.

- The one who is content with less will increase his income with the speed of express.

- Don't look apart inside, look the same outside.

- People fly information rather than planes.

- The good are happy, on the other hand, the lucky ones are hopeful.

- The world has a thousand different states; which one are you from?

- Soap, washes the people, soup feeds the labourer.

- A dishonest person has no validity, neither his preface nor his last word.

- When you think you're a sucker and your friend is cunning, the friendship is over then.

- And the wrongdoer is also in favor of justice, but fot his own Justice.

- This is my wish : May your day be active and your labor be productive.

- He cheated on the strangers, he has set himself up out of angers.

- Even if hard, every exam has something that teaches people.

- On the peaceful hills they crushed the peace.

- Come to the main point, please, be obedient.

- Everyone spends money, and he spends everyone.

- Those who find traces and those who apply them are separate faces.

- Some trusts in his weapon, some in his deity in the brain.

- Don't play with my dreams, let them free, since they have no desire for fee.

- If you spent like I said, you wouldn't be wasted like you said.

- A person must have a challenge to enter every heart.

- To the dog, 'my son', someone said, guess whether his mother or father.

- Every song is a life story not very long.

- If you say it's unbearable, I can't stand, find someone who is almighty to lean against Him.

- Do not let anyone but Allah come in between you with the good you did.

- The needle of some the mother-in-laws' in their hands and the others' on their tongue.

- Suddenly no one falls in love, but I was hit by the blind bullet of love.

- Dhulayha took possession of Joseph, even if she couldn't have him.

- Seasons die too; spring is greetings to the dead of winter and autumn also reads the salute of summer.

- If tongue is diction, the eye is steering.

- Don't think about anything other than the good but don't say no in a bad mood.

- As an incidence, I have never come across any coincidence.

- Don't underestimate yourself too much; there is only one of you in this world.

- In joy, all the characters unite, in anger, they separate from each other.

- A person should be with every move he makes, or else, he should not do it.

- Someone who dreams without borders, what else he doesn't dream about.

- All the dead and alive live in the time.

- Vigilance and accident rarely come across.

- My Lord put wings on me when everyone came to watch my falling.

- At all times, the small birds with wings pass the big one with the long steps.

- The one who pretends to be asleep is craftier than the one who doesn't sleep .

- May my Lord accept me, not so important being either a servant or a stamp.

- The one who was deceived is a fool but cheating one is a devious.

- What you see depends on where you are looking through.

- A person's cleanliness can even be understood in his language.

- There are those who were injured unlike them there are those who also benefit from these injures.

- If you put the little man in the big place, he thinks of you as he himself used to be.

- It is the strength of the wrist that corrects the curve and it's the ability to persuade the wrong one.

- He who is following the footsteps of the devil will surely meet him soon.

- Non-owner property is possible but he who does not own it has no property.

- At your birth, your parents have the right to decide about you, but you do not have the right to choose them.

- He who trusts the devil deactivates his mind.

- A person's human quality is as much as his sense of responsibility.

- The young man who is wrestling with you must be a man of honor, so that you are equal.

- There is a divine pleasure in a divine dispatch.

- Every experience in life is an important capital for the future.

- Even if your cult is the same, your bowl must be different.

- Calamities have two sides, visible and invisible ; the visible side belongs to all humans, but other hidden side is known only by the Lord.

- It is a characteristic of having a mark of horse, but man's mark is useless.

- A person who disguises himself in many guises comes out of a human guise.

- He was content with less that it was not finished, he was so overwhelmed that it is over.

- The distance between us is as far as you are from me, as close as I am to you.

- Honey seller's tongue is like honey, his property is like dog food.

- It is so difficult to see some people that you have to go to heaven to see them.

- Every person has a flaw, every family must have a place to move.

- Those who want to live endeaver, those who are eager to die flutter.

- Ours is not a consanguineous marriage, but the marriage of convenience.

- Some live from the saddlebag, some live for free out of other's bag.

- The person determines his own value with his own personality.

- Give me your heart, and I'll give you my life from start.

- Your hands, your legs, are your charm if you use them for your purpose in the factory or a farm.

- Someone who cries has to be silenced before making him laugh.

- In short, for dynamism, the soil recycling mechanism.

- Loneliness disciplines those who do not appreciate the value of being loved.

- He left me in the lake, however, I realized his intention too late.

- He who oppresses his soul revives his breath.

- . Friends are as like sidewalks; Although there is no organic bond between you and them, you get the feeling of security from them.

- Love is not deceiving but to be mutually convinced.

- Among our friends there are those we give up and there are those whom we pass through.

- If we don't endure for success, in failure, we endure a few times.

- The unscrupulous, the conscience whines when I seeing the oppressed ones.

- Although he has four eyes, all his eyes are on her.

- The true fool is the one who adores mistakes, but not ones who make mistakes.

- As a distance between heaven and us stands only this world.

- Although some smell bad, there are no ugly flowers.

- Trouble will pass, but if it becomes troublesome to you, it will not.

- You say it's my worth, and it becomes your destiny.

- In every person, there are some fears, and sometimes those fears come true with tears.

- One does not need a thousand lies to be considered a liar, only one is enough.

- If you are right, your eyes should confirm what tongue says.

- Neither handcraft doesn't end, nor does anyone else's work which is so hard.

- The enemy speaks of your disaster not by beating, but by praising.

- Some men and women are divided into two; when they are jealous.

- No matter how expensive it is, the food you dislike means nothing in your eyes.

- Our only common ground with him was humanity, and he lost it.

- The stone is heavy in hand, it's deaf on the ground.

- The people with loving hearts connect us to life.

- Even if children know how to eat, they do not know how to feed so do some adults.

- One's humanity is as much as the compassion he carries in his heart.

- He's trouble-free, hassle because he's irresponsible.

- Those who are in an effort to renew cannot be defeated.

- The leaf protects the fruit, but not the branch of it.

- True scholars are the most troubled people on earth.

- The verses of some poems are like embers; they burn the lung of the reader, not his eyes.

- In reality he who is honoring others, in fact mostly 'honors' himself.

- The opponent of the oppressors and the owner of the oppressed is Allah.

- He has no chance of being cured, but he is likely to be culled.

- They want to meet face-to-face, but they have no face.

- May God combine your dreams with your destiny.

- Sometimes the high-pitched voice of some, sometimes the silence of others bothers you.

- Each person's power can be exhausted, but his earthly affairs is not finished.

- Nature of certain events are understood after years and some of them very clear from years ago.

- The more technology gets smarter the more it makes us crazy,

- Every success is a self-confidence renewal story.

- There's only one way, and if that's wrong, then being still is regarded as a move.

- You were nothing without me, therefore you chose me.

- The problems of the waves are always with the shore, they always beat it.

- The farmer lives according to the weather, even if he's not airy.

- Professions are changing in people's eyes, really popular professions are changing.

- Time works in favor of the hardworking employee, also it works against the lazy.

- His mouth is open to everything, his heart is closed to everyone.

- The beginning of the honesty is pain, the end is the crown.

- Manners, rather than knowledge, make man noble.

- An accident occurs when two heedlessness coincide.

- Every house has a cat and a master with tact.

- Some erase the mistake, some digest them, in fact.

- Die, but what you die for must be worth it.

- One purpose, two separate stories to express.

- An intelligent person uses his bitter experience for life, like a spicy sauce.

- life process is connected to automatic; involuntary, it is impossible to stop aging.

- While you are being tested you also test those around you by it.

- Whoever stays with a person without a diameter will be without a diameter, at least with a radius.

- When the valiant is in difficulty case, when the person is in trouble shows its true capacity then.

- Every path to God passes throughout love.

- What we're going through were first dreams and then a war of forces.

- No one is tying me up, but there exist many crying oppressed ones behind my back.

- People take into account the poets more than politicians.

- Looking at them over the years, some mistakes still upset you, while others still make you laugh.

- The nutworm caused irreversible damage to the peasant at present.

- Be the ones who take care of each other with your friends, not be the ones who cheating with someone else.

- Gold is a tin for those who don't understand.

- Have a heart friend but not a false friend.

- The deed we trust most is the time.

- He does it out of spite, not in the name of religion to fight.

- Do not give me an example, set an example for all.

- Ignorance is a sea; nobody can swim in it, but drowns.

- With a drop of urine the sea will not be dirty, but you will be dirty.

- I saw a crack like a string, but until now I have not seen such a thing.

- He who does everything the soul says goes till the hell.

- What troubles have in common is that they all cause troubles.

- One's crying while sleeping is a sign of how close dreams are to reality.

- Our most reliable custodian is time because we leave everything to it.

- Even the prey escapes in front of you but as its preyer cannot escape the death.

- Allah does not look at your hat, He looks at your head.

- You may need a lot to succeed, but the most important thing is your determination to succeed.

- The difference between blind and ungrateful is that one doesn't really see, the other does not consider the good deeds.

- Love is the yeast, it's the fidelity in the heart of a true lover yet, it is a harmful plague in the heart of those who do misunderstand.

- The cat are the zipped version of the lion.

- In life, he who is always living in need, never gets full in deed.

- Some of men are the essance of a man, some are the eyes of a commodity.

- My girlfriend is the only one, but I love a lot.

- Providing that anyone is unique in the world, that is you.

- The person who taps your shoulder is your friend, and the person who leans on your shoulder is your soul.

- The power given to you is to defend, not to chuck away.

- Better be dumb rather than being irreligious.

- The one who doesn't have a crime doesn't have an enemy of any.

- Man makes his mother small first.

- Colors have optals people have fools.

- The heart suffers the pain that we gain.

- The fire of love also burns people but it is smokeless.

- Even though the sea fluctuates a lot, it does not get cold quickly and get angry quickly.

- Even if the relative is like a scorpion, you carry it on your back and stings you all the time .

- Some people live in luxury even if they are not rich. That is, they live in the luxury of mistakes.

- The enemy writes down your failure as a success to his list.

- For everyone the last day, the compulsory direction is doomsday.

- Providing that you despise it every sin is strong enough to overcome you.

- Both eyes cry together because the pain comes from the same source

- This guy's even against himself, why?

- Even a light wind disperses the cloud, but a lead does not penetrate the cloud.

- Those who play on the honor of others are dishonest, even if those are their enemies.

- The one who wrestles with the devil wins, but the one who laughs with him loses.

- Great personalities are like alchemists; they turn every person they deal with into gold.

- Justice is like faith in a way; either it exists or it doesn't… it doesn't have more or less.

- The madman goes backwards, yet a stream does not flow back.

- The matches of hell are your sins.

- If something just stays in the word without action, it is like a product that stays on the shelf not sold.

- The devil is more persistent than our shadows, because the shadow does not enter the darkness or bed with you, but it does.

- Everywhere, the real justice is entrusted to Allah.

- I feel very sorry for those who have no place to stay rather than those who have no place to go. Because those who don't have a place to go may stay in the same place where they are.

- Even though love is described best by poets, death is best represented by the dead himself.

- There is no big or small lie; even the smallest one can deceive a person.

- Some make money with honor, some others make money through honor.

- Even the brave have their weak moments like everyone else. Their weakest moment is the time when they are caught red-handed.

- They even ask for diplomas from unemployed people around here.

- No one likes the privileged one, but everyone wants to be privileged.

- You can also figure out a person's diameter by looking at his enemies.

- What is written with the pen of power of God cannot be known or erased.

- Peace makes every environment it enters happy.

- A bribe-taker has no value, he only has a price.

- Though you made childlike movements, but you couldn't have a child.

- The joy of life of young people, just because they think of beautiful things for future, meanwhile old people's pessimism is because of the possibility that his bad experiences will clutch.

- Consider yourself as a point at some point.

- The eye looks into the eye, the feelings flow into the heart meanwhile.

- You can't draw the line of evil that someone can do but the good he can do is limited.

- A rational man has little margin of decisiveness between what he dreams of and what he performs.

- Not every winged bird can fly, as not every bird with feet can run.

- That ungrateful man ate much of his friend's bread before and after his enmity.

- It's better for you to tell me you've done it once than to tell me you'll do it for a thousand times.

- Being right is like being with God.

- A person who always considers himself right is infallible in his own way.

- When drinking tea, we talk about trivial things, serious issues are discussed while drinking coffee. In other words, there is sincerity in tea and seriousness in coffee.

- Deep wound is not possible with thin stitch, hot tea doesn't come in one gulp from fridge.

- The good as well as the bad have a great contribution to my success.

- Be attached to those who add value to you, not to the one who lies in the mud.

- A good man teaches you something, whereas you learn many things from the bad.

- There are many options on the agenda of determined people, except giving up.

- Love makes a person both childish and mature.

- A person's smile even though his eyes are teary is from the overflowing happiness in his heart.

- A rabbit is a queen without a king among her offsprings.

- Someone whose religin is money will do everything for his religion.

- If you deepen your heedlessness, you will encounter your own stupidity.

- Because of being one the source of pain both eyes cry together.

- The tears in the eyes while peeling onions are not due to the pain in the liver, but because of the onion bitter.

- Some people are gifts, in the meantime some are lifts.

- Now that nafs is your mount, then treat it the way you act the ride.

- That man's hostile attitude took precedence over his humanity.

- Even if they did not commit the crime, the ones who laugh at the oppressed are as guilty as the oppressor.

- He who gives a heart also makes concessions.

- It's a dark night that separates yesterday from today.

- All the effort of the silkworm is to weave a web around itself.

- I am very angry that the holiday seems as if it will never end at first but then it ends so quickly.

- A person who is envious now learn it piece by piece in the near future.

- The most hypocritical tool is the pen; depending on its owner It writes differently on each hand.

- I open an account with some, while I settle accounts with others.

- A teacher should also listen to the parents and the data related to events.

- A man who doesn't like anybody must like only himself.

- If you are at a decoupling between hate and love, choose the love in respect of yourself.

- Cry, cry, cry … until your tears become a lake and then float a boat in the lake, relax… forget everything that tires your mind.

- Even leaders,for some are story heroes or for some are bale of straws.

- In any case before showing reaction give them a plausible reason.

- Like all ants, bees are also sisters.

- Without courage, bondage is inevitable savage.

- Your birth and even your death must carry a message.

- After making all of the mistakes that can be made idiots find the truth.

- Mothers are born as natural teachers; first the teacher of the family, then the entire society.

- The value of health is best known by those who are sick and those who have sick at home.

- Words you produced also wear clothes, but the characters differ according to the person using them.

- The mentor of all evil is the same person: the devil.

- He who has no one to break will eventually break himself.

- The person who goes to every market are called a slut if he's not a salesman.

- Thieves always get caught in their last job because it's their last task.

- Today is not the time for bondage, it is the time for courage.

- A cup of tea is not served without brewing, a horse is not served without saddling the horse.

- A foolish man is a person who has lived a long life and has not learned how to live.

- It is such a thing that its existence is abstract, in addition its thought is hope.

- As long as you give value to the worthless, you become worthless.

- Distance doesn't matter much if you're taking the right step.

- Wings don't make people fly, yet dreams blow people away.

- The son understands his father after he becomes a father, however, it's too late for him because it's his turn to be a father.

- That is a mistake of misconception to think everyone you see as a human.

- Fertile people are similar to a fruit tree; they offer delicious fruits to others while eating mud themselves.

- They are dishonest because they make money through their honor.

- If the birth is a new beginning in life, marriage is the second.

- Helping others and forgiving people strengthen human character.

- There are so many good things to do that you too do one of them.

- Death seems a little distant to a healthy person because before it gets it cripples, withers, and finally puts him on the bed.

- The one who does favour finds goodness, but the form of the favour that comes is slightly in different form.

- Do not rush, mad! don't go fast to death.

- That man's only connection to the sea is that he lives on its edge.

- Look out! not the straight path, but the right path takes people to the destination.

- Don't try to tame the madman, with the insane you will be disciplined.

- The man is so generous that if he moves to the village, he can become a landlord in two days.

- Anyone who does not express a constructive opinion on a job he has no right to criticize.

- Human beings can hide their faces, but never their essence … .

- ID is not enough for some to show, they also have to be asked for a humanity certificate.

- Let the sun hit your forehead, not your belly first, every morning.

- Life is a game from beginning till the end, but you need to look from end to beginning to understand it wholly.

- Telling a lie is acting against your own pure character.

- Positive people put wings on your dreams, nevertheless, negative people break those wings.

- The moon is torn apart because of the sun, and it goes from shape to shape as well.

- Even a drop of water gets smaller as it gets smaller because of its modesty, so much so that Allah puts invisible wings on it in return.

- Bad managers try to get a share of the happiness of the citizen instead of contributing to the happiness.

- Some seem a lion in the image, however, a snake in character.

- If two heedlessness come together, a disaster comes into existance.

- I could not understand whether this announcer is presenting the news or presenting herself.

- God puts those who are confident in himself to such a height that no one can reach him anymore.

- Everyone understands everything from where there the wound is.

- Responding to a word by being silent is heavier than the verbal response.

- The increase in respect for someone over time, but not all of a sudden, shows the depth of that person's personality.

- Even if you're one hundred percent right in any case, you're still slightly guilty.

- According to just everyone's head, there is no world here.

- The good ones come and leave traces, the bad ones go and hand down soot.

- My best favourable ship is a close friendship.

- If you want to know whether the error you made big or small, look at the outcome of it.

- I want an eraser for my mistakes to erase, and I want some attention from you to pay.

- After the fire hit me, I came into recognition that the fire burned where it fell.

- There are many reasons to be angry, but none of them are available.

- The man is in harmony with his name but raw with his tongue.

- Those who are unreliable taught me not everyone can be trusted.

- Personality is like an identity card; when needed it must be shown.

- 993 Psychologically I'm so fit because I was treated.

- My screams put down your cruel king.

- Crises cover up some problems while nudging the others.

- Not always maggots come out by scratching but sometimes troubles come.

- If the left side of him is good, his track and his end will also be good.

- For some people, the distance between wisdom and insanity is only three milimetre long.

- Money has neither a religion nor conscience.

- Everyone collects something, some in his head, others just in his bag.

About the Author

The writer Davut Ersoy was born in 1960 in Yozgat in the country side and started his primary education in Akdağmadeni town. Later on, he moved to Zonguldak so completed his secondary education there, After graduating from Gazi University he taught English in several cities in Turkey; Ordu, Amasya and Zonguldak. The process of teaching English lasted for 28 years. He also has his Master's Degree. He was interested indifferent branches of literature amateurish at a very young age, especially poetry. Published two books : CONTEMPARY APHORISMS, WISE COUPLETS. As former English teacher, newly retired one he takes great deal of time different branch of literature; poetry, aphorism. He's married and father of an only child.

www.ingramcontent.com/pod-product-compliance
Lightning Source LLC
LaVergne TN
LVHW011729060526
838200LV00051B/3092